AIN'T NO BAD JOKE LIKE A

DAD

JOKE

Published by Willow Creek Press, Inc.
P.O. Box 147, Minocqua, Wisconsin 54548

Printed in the United States

AIN'T NO BAD JOKE LIKE A

DAD JOKE

☒ WILLOW CREEK PRESS®

WHAT DID THE FISH SAY WHEN HE SWAM INTO A WALL? DAM.

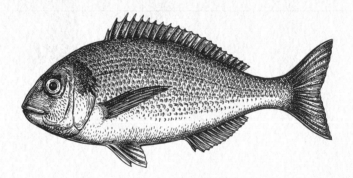

WHAT DID THE GRAPE SAY WHEN IT GOT CRUSHED? NOTHING, IT JUST LET OUT A LITTLE WINE.

WHAT DO YOU CALL AN
ALLIGATOR IN A VEST?
AN INVESTIGATOR.

BEST PRESENT THIS YEAR WAS A BROKEN DRUM. YOU CAN'T BEAT THAT!

ALL CHEMISTS KNOW THAT ALCOHOL IS ALWAYS A SOLUTION.

BECOMING A VEGETARIAN IS ONE BIG MISSED STEAK.

ACCORDING TO MY KIDS, DAD JOKES ARE NOT COOL FOR A-PARENT REASONS.

ARE YOU FREE TOMORROW? NO, I'M EXPENSIVE. SORRY.

A PLATEAU IS THE HIGHEST FORM OF FLATTERY.

BIG SALE ON ROWING PADDLES AT MY LOCAL SHOP. IT'S QUITE AN OAR DEAL.

BASKETBALL PLAYERS ARE REALLY MESSY EATERS. THEY ARE ALWAYS DRIBBLING.

DID YOU SEE THE DOG'S NEW OUTFIT? IT WAS QUITE FETCHING!

BROKEN GUITAR FOR SALE. NO STRINGS ATTACHED.

DID YOU HEAR ABOUT THE
ANXIOUS SEAMSTRESS?
SHE'S ON PINS
AND NEEDLES.

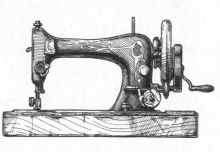

DID YOU HEAR ABOUT THE ITALIAN CHEF WHO DIED? HE PASTA-WAY.

DID YOU HEAR ABOUT THE SHRIMP THAT WENT TO THE PRAWN'S COCKTAIL PARTY? HE PULLED A MUSSEL.

A GOLF BALL IS A GOLF BALL NO MATTER HOW YOU PUTT IT.

DON'T TRUST ATOMS. THEY MAKE UP EVERYTHING!

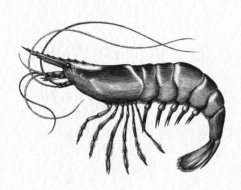

DID YOU ADOPT YOUR DOG? NO, HE'S MY BIOLOGICAL DOG.

DID YOU HEAR THE RUMOR ABOUT BUTTER? WELL, I'M NOT GOING TO SPREAD IT.

DID YOU HEAR ABOUT THE GROUP OF BABIES THAT FORMED A GANG? THEY HANG OUT IN THEIR CRIB.

**FOUND A SPIDER IN MY SHOES...
HE LOOKED SILLY. THEY WERE
WAY TOO BIG FOR HIM!**

WHAT DO YOU CALL A COW WITH NO LEGS? GROUND BEEF.

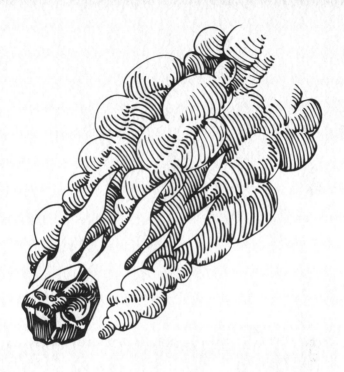

WHAT DO PLANETS LIKE TO READ? COMET BOOKS!

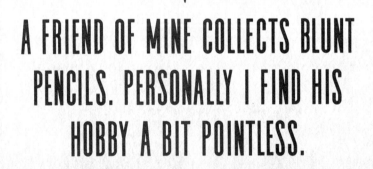

A FRIEND OF MINE COLLECTS BLUNT PENCILS. PERSONALLY I FIND HIS HOBBY A BIT POINTLESS.

A DETECTIVE WAS RUSHED TO THE ER. HE ACCIDENTALLY POKED HIS PRIVATE EYE.

APPLE IS DESIGNING A NEW AUTOMATIC CAR. BUT THEY'RE HAVING TROUBLE INSTALLING WINDOWS!

GERMAN SAUSAGE JOKES ARE JUST THE WURST.

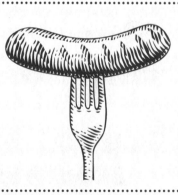

A SHIP CARRYING RED PAINT HAS COLLIDED WITH A SHIP CARRYING BLUE PAINT. BOTH CREWS ARE SAID TO BE MAROONED.

A RABBIT USED TO COME UP TO MY FRONT YARD EVERY DAY FOR FOOD, BUT HASN'T SHOWN UP IN A WEEK. NOW IT'S JUST SOME BUNNY I USED TO KNOW.

HAPPINESS COMES FROM WITHIN. THAT'S WHY IT FEELS SO GOOD TO FART.

HOW DO BILLBOARDS TALK? SIGN LANGUAGE.

HAVE YOU HEARD ABOUT THE PRISONER WHO MAKES GOOD COCKTAILS? HE'S BEHIND BARS NOW!

ENGLAND DOESN'T HAVE A KIDNEY BANK, BUT IT DOES HAVE A LIVERPOOL.

6:30 IS THE BEST TIME ON A CLOCK... HANDS DOWN.

HOW DOES THE MOON CUT HIS HAIR? ECLIPSE IT!

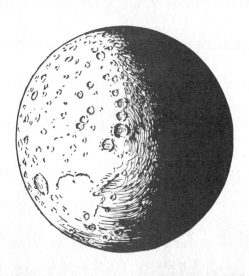

**HOW DO YOU GET A
SQUIRREL TO LIKE YOU?
ACT LIKE YOU'RE NUTS.**

I INVENTED A
NEW WORD:
PLAGIARISM!

I DON'T TRUST STAIRS. THEY'RE ALWAYS UP TO SOMETHING.

HOW DO YOU FIND WILL SMITH IN THE SNOW? LOOK FOR THE FRESH PRINTS.

HOW DO MINECRAFT PLAYERS CELEBRATE? THEY THROW BLOCK PARTIES!

I BOUGHT A BOAT BECAUSE IT WAS FOR SAIL.

I BECAME
HOOKED ON
AUCTIONS
AFTER ONLY
GOING ONCE...
GOING TWICE...

I TRIED
TO DRAW
A CIRCLE,
BUT IT WAS
POINTLESS.

I KNEW A GUY WHO COLLECTED
CANDY CANES, THEY WERE
ALL IN MINT CONDITION.

I JUST READ A GREAT BOOK ON THE HISTORY
OF GLUE, I COULDN'T PUT IT DOWN.

WHY DID THE ORANGE STOP
HALF WAY UP THE HILL?
IT RAN OUT OF JUICE.

HOW WAS ROME SPLIT IN TWO? WITH A PAIR OF CAESARS.

I USED TO HATE FACIAL HAIR.
BUT THEN IT GREW ON ME.

IF A CHILD REFUSES TO SLEEP DURING NAP TIME, ARE THEY GUILTY OF RESISTING A REST?

I MADE A PLAYLIST FOR HIKING.
IT HAS MUSIC FROM PEANUTS,
THE CRANBERRIES, AND EMINEM.
I CALL IT MY TRAIL MIX.

I WENT ON A ONCE—
IN—A—LIFETIME
VACATION.
NEVER AGAIN.

WHAT DO YOU CALL A PONY
WITH A COUGH? A LITTLE HOARSE.

I OWN A PENCIL THAT USED
TO BE OWNED BY WILLIAM
SHAKESPEARE, BUT HE CHEWED
IT A LOT. NOW I CAN'T TELL
IF IT'S 2B OR NOT 2B.

I'VE BEEN LOOKING FOR SOME
NEW HUNTING GEAR. GOOD
CAMOUFLAGE IS HARD TO FIND.

IF YOU EVER FEEL COLD JUST STAND IN A CORNER. THEY'RE USUALLY AROUND 90 DEGREES.

ICE HOCKEY... WHAT A COOL SPORT.

I WANTED TO LEARN HOW TO DRIVE A STICK SHIFT, BUT I COULDN'T FIND A MANUAL.

I'M ON A SEAFOOD DIET. EVERY TIME I SEE FOOD, I EAT IT.

I WROTE A SONG ABOUT A TORTILLA. WELL ACTUALLY, IT'S MORE OF A WRAP.

LONG FAIRY TALES HAVE A TENDENCY TO DRAGON.

PRICES FOR CHIMNEYS HAVE GONE THROUGH THE ROOF!

I SAW A MAN WITH A TROLLEY FULL OF HORSESHOES AND RABBIT'S FEET EARLIER TRYING TO GET UP A HILL. I THOUGHT HE'S PUSHING HIS LUCK.

I'M NO CHEETAH...YOU'RE LION!

MY BOSS ASKED ME TO ATTACH TWO PIECES OF WOOD TOGETHER. I NAILED IT!

PEANUT BUTTER
JOKES AREN'T
FUNNY UNTIL
YOU SPREAD THEM.

I WATCHED A
DOCUMENTARY
LAST NIGHT
ABOUT HOW
SHIPS ARE MADE.
RIVETING.

MY WIFE GAVE ME A LEAFLET
ON ANGER MANAGEMENT...
HOPE I DON'T LOSE IT!

IF YOU THROW A PENCIL UP IN
THE AIR IS IT STILL STATIONERY?

I WENT TO THE DOCTOR TO
TELL HIM ABOUT MY CRAVING
FOR COLLECTING IPADS.
HE GAVE ME SOME TABLETS.

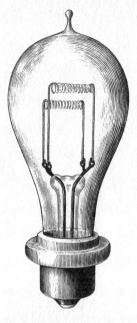

**MOST PEOPLE ARE SHOCKED
WHEN THEY FIND OUT HOW
BAD AN ELECTRICIAN I AM.**

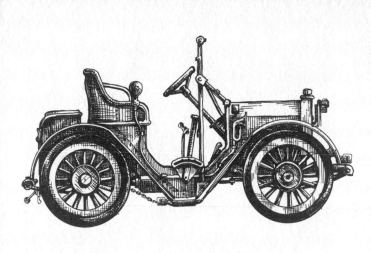

MY CAR ONLY WORKS EVERY
OTHER DAY. I THINK IT
MIGHT BE THE ALTERNATOR.

MY FRIEND'S BAKERY
BURNED DOWN LAST NIGHT.
NOW HIS BUSINESS IS TOAST.

I WOULDN'T BUY ANYTHING WITH VELCRO. IT'S A TOTAL RIP-OFF.

MY DOG'S NOT FAT. HE'S JUST A LITTLE HUSKY.

MY NEIGHBOR PLANTED DOGWOOD TREES IN HIS FRONT YARD. I'M NOT A HUGE FAN OF THE BARK.

I TOOK MY ACCORDION TO BE REPAIRED. THE GUY SAID HE WOULD TRY TO SQUEEZE IT IN.

NEVER MARRY A TENNIS PLAYER. LOVE MEANS NOTHING TO THEM.

MY NEW GIRLFRIEND WORKS AT THE ZOO. I THINK SHE'S A KEEPER.

I USED TO WORK IN A BLANKET FACTORY, BUT IT FOLDED.

I WAS HAPPY TO HEAR THAT HUMPTY DUMPTY HAD A GREAT FALL... AFTER SUCH A LOUSY SPRING AND SUMMER.

SOME AQUATIC MAMMALS AT THE ZOO ESCAPED. IT WAS OTTER CHAOS!

WHAT DO YOU CALL A MAN WITH A HAT MADE OF HOUSEHOLD TOOLS? HANDY CAPPED.

I WENT BIRD HUNTING WITH MY SON. IT WAS QUITE PHEASANT.

THE INVENTOR OF THE USB STICK HAS DIED. THANKS FOR THE MEMORY.

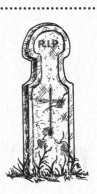

SO WHAT IF I CAN'T SPELL ARMAGEDDON? IT'S NOT THE END OF THE WORLD.

THE WEDDING WAS SO BEAUTIFUL. EVEN THE CAKE WAS IN TIERS.

WHAT ANIMAL NEEDS TO WEAR A WIG? A BALD EAGLE.

THERE'S A NEW TYPE OF BROOM OUT. IT'S SWEEPING THE NATION.

SIMBA WAS WALKING SO SLOWLY I TOLD HIM TO MUFASA.

THERE'S A FINE LINE BETWEEN NUMERATOR AND DENOMINATOR.

WHY DID THE FISH GET BAD GRADES? BECAUSE IT WAS BELOW SEA LEVEL.

THE MIDDLE AGES WERE
CALLED THE DARK AGES
BECAUSE THERE WERE
TOO MANY KNIGHTS.

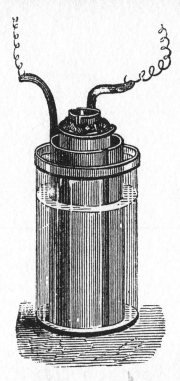

TODAY I GAVE MY DEAD
BATTERIES AWAY. THEY
WERE FREE OF CHARGE.

WHAT DID ONE FLAG
SAY TO THE OTHER?
NOTHING, IT JUST WAVED.

**SCIENTISTS HAVE JUST COMPLETED
A STUDY INTO THE EFFECTS
OF ALCOHOL ON WALKING.
THE RESULT WAS STAGGERING.**

CORDUROY PILLOWS ARE MAKING HEADLINES.

TO THE GUY WHO INVENTED ZERO, THANKS FOR NOTHING.

WHAT DID ONE MATH BOOK SAY TO THE OTHER? I'VE GOT SO MANY PROBLEMS.

WHY DID THE BELT GET THROWN IN JAIL? HE HELD UP A PAIR OF PANTS.

WHAT DID THE DUCK SAY WHEN SHE PURCHASED NEW LIPSTICK? PUT IT ON MY BILL!

TOWELS CAN'T TELL JOKES. THEY HAVE A DRY SENSE OF HUMOR.

A GUY TRIED TO SELL ME A COFFIN. I TOLD HIM THAT'S THE LAST THING I NEED.

WHAT DO CATS WEAR TO SLEEP? PAWJAMAS!

WHY WAS THE MIME INCARCERATED? HE COMMITTED UNSPEAKABLE CRIMES.

WHAT DO ALEXANDER THE GREAT AND WINNIE THE POOH HAVE IN COMMON? THE SAME MIDDLE NAME.

DO YOU KNOW WHY THE CLAM MURDERED THE OYSTER? SHELLFISH REASONS.

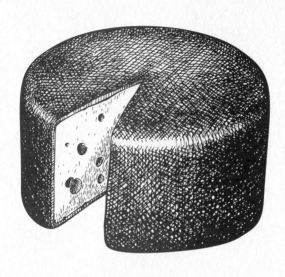

A CHEESE FACTORY HAS
EXPLODED IN FRANCE...
THERE'S DE BRIE EVERYWHERE!

DON'T USE DOUBLE NEGATIVES. THEY'RE A BIG NO NO.

WHAT DO YOU CALL A TIRED SKELETON? THE GRIM SLEEPER.

WHAT DO YOU CALL A CAN OPENER THAT DOESN'T WORK? A CAN'T OPENER!

MY UNCLE WAS CRUSHED BY A PIANO.... HIS FUNERAL WAS VERY LOW KEY.

WHAT DO YOU CALL A FRENCHMAN IN SANDALS? PHILLIPE FLOPPE.

I USED TO BE ADDICTED TO TIME TRAVEL. BUT THAT'S ALL IN THE PAST NOW.

IT TAKES GUTS TO BE AN ORGAN DONOR.

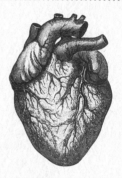

WHAT DO OLYMPIC SPRINTERS EAT BEFORE A RACE? NOTHING. THEY FAST.

WHAT DO CONSTRUCTION WORKERS DO AT PARTIES? THEY RAISE THE ROOF.

MY WIFE BLOCKED ME
ON FACEBOOK BECAUSE
I POST TOO MANY BIRD
PUNS. WELL, TOUCAN
PLAY AT THAT GAME.

How many tickles
does it take to make
an octopus laugh?
10-tickles.

WHAT DID THE BUFFALO SAY TO HER CHILD AS HE LEFT FOR SCHOOL? BISON.

DID YOU HEAR ABOUT THE GUY WHO EVAPORATED? HE'LL BE MIST!

HOW MUCH DO DUMPLINGS WEIGH? WONTON.

TO THE PERSON WHO STOLE MY PLACE IN THE QUEUE. I'M AFTER YOU NOW.

WHEN DOES A JOKE BECOME A DAD JOKE? WHEN IT BECOMES APPARENT.

WHAT DO YOU CALL A HAPPY COWBOY? A JOLLY RANCHER.

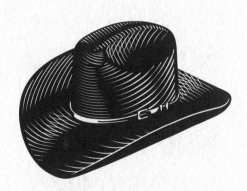

WHAT KIND OF CHEESE ISN'T YOURS? NACHO CHEESE.

WHAT DO YOU CALL A SAD STRAWBERRY? A BLUEBERRY.

WHAT DO YOU CALL A STUDENT WHO DOESN'T LIKE MATH CLASS? CALCU-HATER.

WHAT DO YOU CALL A TURTLE WHO TAKES UP PHOTOGRAPHY? A SNAPPING TURTLE.

WHAT DO YOU CALL A KNIGHT WHO IS AFRAID TO FIGHT? SIR RENDER.

I HAD TO FIRE THE GUY I HIRED TO MOW MY LAWN. HE JUST DIDN'T CUT IT.

WHAT DO YOU GET WHEN THE QUEEN OF ENGLAND FARTS?
A NOBLE GAS.

WHAT DOES TONY HAWK USE TO LANDSCAPE HIS YARD? FACE PLANTS.

WHAT EXPLORER WAS THE BEST AT HIDE AND SEEK? MARCO POLO.

WHAT DOES A THESAURUS EAT FOR BREAKFAST? SYNONYM TOAST CRUNCH.

WHAT KIND OF SHOES DOES A FROG WEAR? OPEN TOAD.

DID YOU HEAR ABOUT THE BIG LEGO SALE? PEOPLE WERE LINED UP FOR BLOCKS.

MY WIFE WAS MAD AT ME BECAUSE I'M LAZY. I DIDN'T EVEN DO ANYTHING!

WHAT KIND OF LIGHTS DID NOAH HAVE ON THE ARK? FLOOD LIGHTS!

WHAT HAS FOUR WHEELS AND FLIES? A GARBAGE TRUCK.

WHAT IS A GOLFER'S WORST NIGHTMARE? THE BOGEYMAN.

WHAT DOES C.S. LEWIS KEEP AT THE BACK OF HIS WARDROBE? NARNIA BUSINESS!

**WHAT KIND OF TREE
FITS IN YOUR HAND?
A PALM TREE.**

WHAT WAS THE CAT'S FAVORITE SUBJECT IN SCHOOL? HISSSSTORY!

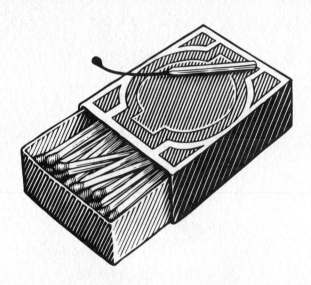

I JOINED A DATING
SITE FOR ARSONISTS.
I'VE BEEN GETTING
A LOT OF MATCHES.

WHAT SHOULD A LAWYER ALWAYS WEAR TO COURT? A GOOD LAWSUIT!

WHERE DO FISH KEEP THEIR MONEY? IN THE RIVER BANK.

I GREW FACIAL HAIR WITHOUT TELLING ANYONE. IT'S MY SECRET 'STACHE.

WHAT KIND OF HEADACHES DO SELFISH WHEAT FARMERS GET? MY GRAINS!

WHERE DO FOOTBALL PLAYERS GO SHOPPING IN THE OFF-SEASON? THE TACKLE SHOP.

WHERE DO HAMBURGERS GO DANCING? A MEATBALL.

WHAT KIND OF MUSIC DO BALLOONS HATE? POP.

MY WIFE SAYS I'M THE CHEAPEST MAN IN THE WORLD. I'M NOT BUYING IT.

WHERE DO MILKSHAKES COME FROM? NERVOUS COWS!

WHY ARE DOGS LIKE PHONES? BECAUSE THEY HAVE COLLAR IDS.

WHY DID THE BANANA GO TO THE DOCTOR? BECAUSE IT WASN'T PEELING WELL.

WHY ARE ELEVATOR JOKES SO CLASSIC AND GOOD? THEY WORK ON MANY LEVELS.

WHY DID THE COOKIE GO TO THE DOCTOR? BECAUSE HE FELT CRUMMY.

WHERE SHOULD A DOG NEVER GO SHOPPING? A FLEA MARKET.

WHY DID SHAKESPEARE'S WIFE WALK OUT ON HIM? SHE WAS SICK OF ALL THE DRAMAS.

WHERE WAS THE DECLARATION OF INDEPENDENCE SIGNED? AT THE BOTTOM!

WHAT IS THE MOST EXPENSIVE FISH IN THE WORLD? THE GOLDFISH.

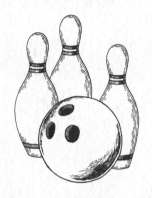

WHY DO BOWLING PINS HAVE SUCH A HARD LIFE? THEY'RE ALWAYS GETTING KNOCKED DOWN.

WHY DID THE CENTER WALK OFF THE FIELD? THE QUARTERBACK TOLD HIM TO HIKE.

WHY DID THE WHARF BREAK? TOO MUCH PIER PRESSURE.

WHY DIDN'T THE CAT GO TO THE VET? HE WAS FELINE FINE!

WHY DID THE DOG CHASE HIS OWN TAIL? HE WAS TRYING TO MAKE BOTH ENDS MEET!

WHY DID THE GOLFER NEED NEW SOCKS? BECAUSE THERE WAS A HOLE IN ONE.

WHAT IS A TREE'S FAVORITE DRINK? ROOT BEER.

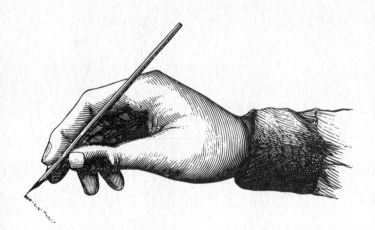

WHICH HAND IS BETTER TO WRITE WITH? NEITHER. IT IS BETTER TO WRITE WITH A PEN.

How do you stop an astronaut's baby from crying? You rocket!

WHERE DO YOU LEARN TO MAKE ICE CREAM? SUNDAE SCHOOL.

WHY DO COMPUTERS NEVER FALL ASLEEP? THEY'RE TOO WIRED.

WHY DO GOLFERS HATE CAKE? BECAUSE THEY MIGHT GET A SLICE.

WHY DO MATH TEACHERS MAKE GOOD DANCERS? BECAUSE THEY HAVE ALGORITHM.

WHY WAS THE COOKIE SAD? BECAUSE HIS MOM WAS A WAFER SO LONG.

WHY ARE FROGS SO HAPPY? THEY EAT WHATEVER BUGS THEM.

WHY DO HAMBURGERS GO TO THE GYM? TO GET BETTER BUNS.

WHY WAS WW2 SO SLOW? BECAUSE THEY WERE STALIN.

I'M READING A HORROR BOOK IN BRAILLE. SOMETHING BAD IS GOING TO HAPPEN. I CAN FEEL IT.

WHY WAS THE STADIUM SO COLD? THERE WERE A LOT OF FANS.

WHY WERE BIKES SUSPENDED FROM SCHOOL? THEY SPOKE TOO MUCH.

THERE'S SOMETHING WRONG WITH THIS CHICKEN. IT TASTES FOWL.

CAN ANYONE TELL ME WHAT "IDK" MEANS? EVERY TIME I ASK SOMEONE, THEY SAY "I DON'T KNOW."

YOU REALLY SHOULDN'T BE INTIMIDATED BY ADVANCED MATH... IT'S EASY AS PI!

WHY DOES BATMAN CARRY A BASEBALL BAT? BECAUSE HE'S THE BATMAN.

HOW MANY BONES ARE IN A HAND? A HANDFUL.

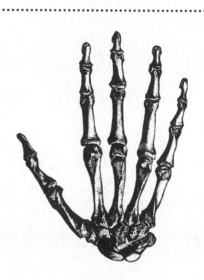

MY BOSS TOLD ME TO HAVE A GOOD DAY. SO I WENT HOME.

WHY WAS THE SAND WET? BECAUSE THE SEA WEED.

WHAT WASHES UP ON REALLY SMALL BEACHES? MICRO-WAVES!

WHY WAS THE PICTURE SENT TO JAIL? IT WAS FRAMED.

WHY AREN'T DOGS GOOD DANCERS? THEY HAVE TWO LEFT FEET.

WHY ARE STORIES ABOUT NASCAR SO SATISFYING? BECAUSE THEY ALWAYS COME FULL CIRCLE.

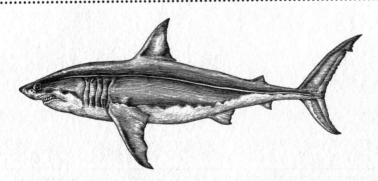

WHAT DO SHARKS SAY WHEN SOMETHING COOL HAPPENS? JAWESOME!

HOW MANY APPLES
GROW ON A TREE?
ALL OF THEM.

I JUST WATCHED A
PROGRAM ABOUT BEAVERS.
IT WAS THE BEST DAM
PROGRAM I'VE EVER SEEN!

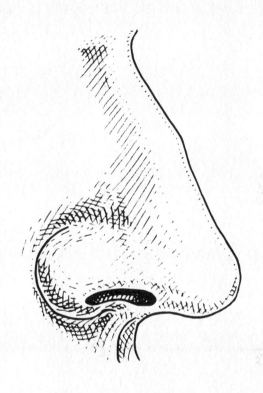

**WHY CAN'T YOUR NOSE
BE 12 INCHES LONG?
BECAUSE THEN IT
WOULD BE A FOOT.**

DAD, DID YOU GET A HAIRCUT? NO I GOT THEM ALL CUT.

IS THIS POOL SAFE FOR DIVING? IT DEEP ENDS.

HAVE YOU HEARD OF THE BAND 1023MB? THEY HAVEN'T GOT A GIG YET.

WANT TO HEAR A JOKE ABOUT PAPER? NEVER MIND, IT'S TEARABLE.

I'M NEVER AGAIN DONATING MONEY TO ANYONE COLLECTING FOR A MARATHON. THEY JUST TAKE THE MONEY AND RUN.

WHAT DO YOU GET WHEN YOU CROSS AN ELEPHANT AND A POTATO? MASHED POTATO.

HOW DO YOU DROWN A HIPSTER?
PUT HIM IN THE MAINSTREAM.

MY WIFE SAYS I ONLY HAVE 2 FAULTS. I DON'T LISTEN—AND SOMETHING ELSE...

WHY ARE IPHONE CHARGERS NOT CALLED APPLE JUICE?

WHY WAS GANDOLF ALWAYS SMOKING THAT PIPE? HE HAD A BAD HOBBIT!

WHY DID THE DEVELOPER GO BROKE? BECAUSE HE USED UP ALL HIS CACHE.

DID YOU HEAR ABOUT THE MONKEYS WHO SHARED AN AMAZON ACCOUNT? THEY WERE PRIME MATES.

WHAT'S THE BEST TIME TO GO TO THE DENTIST? TOOTH-HURTY.

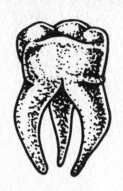

WHERE DOES A BOAT GO WHEN IT'S SICK? TO THE DOCK!

WHAT DID THE PINE TREES WEAR TO THE LAKE? SWIMMING TRUNKS!

WHAT DO YOU CALL A FAT PSYCHIC? A FOUR CHIN TELLER.

DID YOU HEAR THE ONE ABOUT THE GERM? NEVER MIND. I DON'T WANT TO SPREAD IT AROUND.

DID YOU HEAR ABOUT
THE SENSITIVE BURGLAR?
HE TAKES THINGS PERSONALLY.

WHERE DO MONKEYS GO TO GRAB A BEER? THE MONKEY BARS!

WHAT GAME DOES THE SKY LOVE TO PLAY? TWISTER.

WHY DID THE PIG GET HIRED BY THE RESTAURANT? HE WAS REALLY GOOD AT BACON.

DON'T WORRY IF YOU MISS A GYM SESSION... EVERYTHING WILL WORK OUT.

WHAT'S ANOTHER NAME FOR A SLEEPING BAG? A NAP SACK.

**WHY DID THE LION EAT
THE TIGHT-ROPE WALKER?
HE WANTED A WELL-
BALANCED MEAL.**

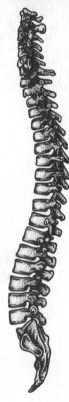

I'M THINKING ABOUT REMOVING MY SPINE... I FEEL LIKE IT'S ONLY HOLDING ME BACK.

WHY DO THE FRENCH EAT SNAILS? CAUSE THEY DON'T LIKE FAST FOOD.

HOW DO TREES ACCESS THE INTERNET? THEY LOG IN.

WHAT DO BIRDS GIVE OUT ON HALLOWEEN? TWEETS.

I DON'T MEAN TO BRAG BUT MY BANK JUST SENT ME AN EMAIL SAYING THAT I AM OUTSTANDING!

WHEN YOU HAVE A BLADDER INFECTION... URINE TROUBLE.

WHAT DID ONE VOLCANO SAY TO THE OTHER VOLCANO? I LAVA YOU!

WHY DID THE COMPUTER SHOW UP AT WORK LATE? IT HAD A HARD DRIVE.

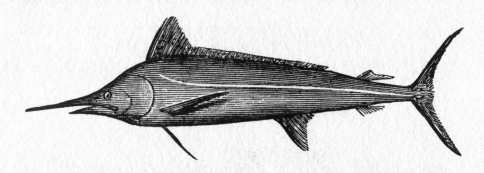

WHAT DID THE SWORDFISH SAY TO THE MARLIN? YOU'RE LOOKING SHARP.

WHY AREN'T KOALAS ACTUAL BEARS? THE DON'T MEET THE KOALAFICATIONS.

WHERE DID NOAH KEEP HIS BEES? IN HIS ARK HIVES.

5/4 OF PEOPLE ADMIT THAT THEY'RE BAD WITH FRACTIONS.

WHERE CAN YOU FIND AN OCEAN WITHOUT WATER? ON A MAP!

I WAS GOING TO START
A BOURBON COMPANY,
BUT I HEARD IT'S
WHISKEY BUSINESS.

WHY DID THE FISH BLUSH? BECAUSE IT SAW THE LAKE'S BOTTOM.

WHAT TRAVELS AROUND THE WORLD BUT STAYS IN ONE CORNER? A STAMP!

WHY DID CINDERELLA GET KICKED OFF THE SOCCER TEAM? BECAUSE SHE RAN AWAY FROM THE BALL.

WHERE DOES THE ELECTRIC CORD GO TO SHOP? THE OUTLET MALL.

WHAT DO YOU DO WITH A DEAD CHEMIST? YOU BARIUM.

WHAT DID THE CROSS-EYED TEACHER SAY? I CAN'T CONTROL MY PUPILS.

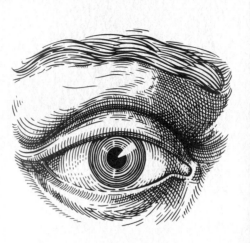

HAVE YOU HEARD ABOUT THE PREGNANT BED BUG? SHE'S GOING TO HAVE HER BABY IN THE SPRING.

WHY DIDN'T THE SAILORS PLAY CARDS? BECAUSE THE CAPTAIN WAS STANDING ON THE DECK.

WHAT KIND OF WHISKY DOES A BUNNY DRINK? HOP SCOTCH.

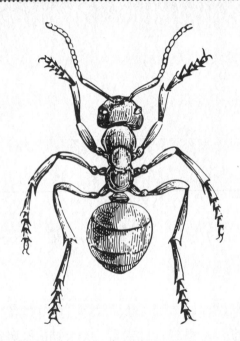

**WHY DON'T ANTS GET SICK?
THEY HAVE ANTY-BODIES.**

I'M THINKING OF
BECOMING A HITMAN...
I HEARD THEY MAKE A KILLING.

CAN I TELL
YOU A
CAT JOKE?
JUST KITTEN!

WHAT NAILS
DO CARPENTERS
HATE TO HIT?
FINGERNAILS.

WHY DID FROSTY ASK FOR A DIVORCE?
HIS WIFE WAS A TOTAL FLAKE.

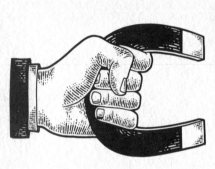

WHAT DID THE MAGNET
SAY TO THE OTHER
MAGNET? I FIND YOU
VERY ATTRACTIVE!

WHAT CAUSES SOME BOATS
TO BECOME PARTY BOATS?
PIER PRESSURE.

WHAT DID THE FISHERMAN
SAY TO THE MAGICIAN?
PICK A COD, ANY COD.

**WHAT DO YOU CALL
A SLEEPING BULL?
A BULLDOZER.**

WHY DID THE POOR MAN SELL YEAST? TO RAISE SOME DOUGH.

WHAT DO YOU CALL A DOG IN THE WINTER? A CHILI DOG!

WHY DID THE PILLOW GO TO THE DOCTOR? HE WAS FEELING ALL STUFFED UP!

NOBODY HAS SEEN THE ZAMBONI DRIVER. BUT I'M SURE HE'LL RESURFACE EVENTUALLY.

WHY DO HUMMINGBIRDS HUM? BECAUSE THEY DON'T KNOW THE WORDS.

WHY DID THE MAN TAKE TOILET PAPER TO THE PARTY? BECAUSE HE WAS A PARTY POOPER.

PEOPLE ARE MAKING TOO MANY APOCALYPSE JOKES... IT'S LIKE THEY THINK THERE'S NO TOMORROW.

I WAS THINKING ABOUT MOVING TO MOSCOW... BUT THERE'S NO POINT IN RUSSIAN INTO THINGS.

WHAT DO YOU CALL A GUY WHO NEVER FARTS IN PUBLIC? A PRIVATE TUTOR.

HOW DO BIRDS FLY? THEY JUST WING IT.

WHY ARE HAIRDRESSERS NEVER LATE FOR WORK? BECAUSE THEY KNOW ALL THE SHORT CUTS.

WHERE DID THE COW TAKE HIS DATE? THE MOOOVIES.

HOW DO YOU MAKE A TISSUE DANCE? PUT A LITTLE BOOGIE IN IT.

WHAT DO YOU CALL A GUY WITH A RUBBER TOE? ROBERTO.

CAN A MATCH BOX? NO, BUT A TIN CAN.

WHAT DO YOU CALL A PILE OF CATS? A MEOWTAIN.

WHAT DO YOU CALL TWO FAT PEOPLE HAVING A CHAT? A HEAVY DISCUSSION.

HOW WAS THE SNOW GLOBE FEELING AFTER THE SCARY STORY? A LITTLE SHAKEN.

WHY COULDN'T THE
BICYCLE STAND UP?
BECAUSE IT WAS
TWO TIRED!

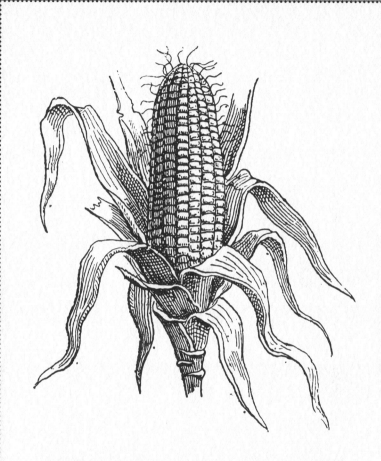

**WHAT DID THE BABY CORN
SAY TO THE MAMA CORN?
WHERE'S POP CORN?**

HOW DO SNAILS FIGHT? THEY SLUG IT OUT.

WHAT GOES UP WHEN THE RAIN COMES DOWN? AN UMBRELLA.

WHAT DID THE SCHIZOPHRENIC BOOKKEEPER SAY? I HEAR INVOICES.

WHY DID THE CLYDESDALE GIVE THE PONY A GLASS OF WATER? BECAUSE HE WAS A LITTLE HORSE.

WHAT DOES A NUT SAY WHEN IT SNEEZES? CASHEW.

WHAT WAS LUDWIG VAN BEETHOVEN'S FAVORITE FRUIT? BA-NA-NA-NA.

**DID YOU HEAR ABOUT
THE T–REX WHO SELLS
GUNS? HE'S A SMALL
ARMS DEALER.**

WHAT DO YOU CALL A PIG
THAT DOES KARATE?
A PORK CHOP.

WHAT DID THE LEFT EYE SAY TO THE RIGHT EYE?
BETWEEN YOU AND ME SOMETHING SMELLS.

WHY COULDN'T
DRACULA'S WIFE
GET TO SLEEP?
BECAUSE OF
HIS COFFIN.

I ATE A CLOCK YESTERDAY...
IT WAS VERY TIME CONSUMING.

WHY DID THE ELEPHANTS
KEEP GETTING KICKED OUT
OF THE POOL? THEY KEPT
DROPPING THEIR TRUNKS!

WHAT DID THE BEAVER SAY TO THE TREE?
IT'S BEEN NICE GNAWING YOU.

HOW DO YOU MAKE A SWISS ROLL? PUSH HIM DOWN THE MOUNTAIN.

THE ENERGIZER BUNNY WAS ARRESTED ON A CHARGE OF BATTERY.

WHAT DID THE MAMA COW SAY TO THE BABY COW? "IT'S PASTURE BEDTIME."

WHAT DO CARS EAT ON THEIR TOAST? TRAFFIC JAM.

WHY COULDN'T THE LEOPARD PLAY HIDE AND SEEK? BECAUSE HE WAS ALWAYS SPOTTED.

WHAT DO YOU DO IF ATTACKED BY A CLAN OF CLOWNS? GO FOR THE JUGGLER.

HOW DID THE HIPSTER BURN HIS MOUTH? HE ATE PIZZA BEFORE IT WAS COOL.

WHAT'S BROWN AND STICKY? A STICK.

WHAT DID ONE TOILET ROLL SAY TO THE OTHER TOILET ROLL? "PEOPLE KEEP RIPPING ME OFF!"

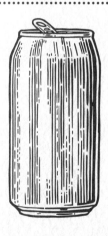 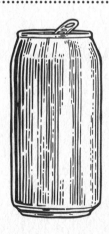

WHY DID THE CAN CRUSHER QUIT HIS JOB? BECAUSE IT WAS SODA PRESSING.

WHY DON'T THEY PLAY POKER IN THE JUNGLE? TOO MANY CHEETAHS.

WHAT DID THE CAKE SAY TO THE FORK? WANT A PIECE OF ME?

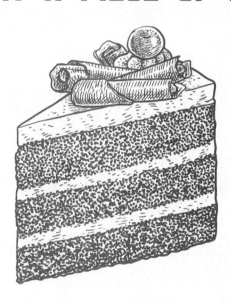

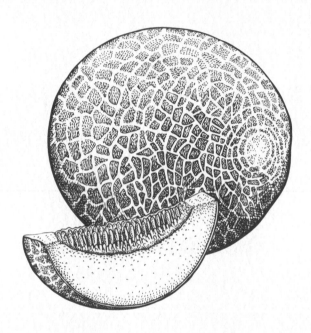

WHY DIDN'T THE MELONS GET MARRIED? BECAUSE THEY CANTALOUPE.

WHAT KIND OF SHOES DO NINJAS WEAR? SNEAKERS.

THE PAST, PRESENT, AND FUTURE WALKED INTO A BAR... IT WAS TENSE.

WANNA HEAR A JOKE ABOUT A STONE? NEVERMIND, I WILL JUST SKIP THAT ONE.

WHAT DO YOU SAY TO A LOLLIPOP WHEN YOU THROW IT AWAY? "SO LONG SUCKER!"

HOW DO YOU TURN WHITE CHOCOLATE INTO DARK CHOCOLATE? TURN OFF THE LIGHT.

HOW DO YOU FIX A BROKEN TUBA? WITH A TUBA GLUE.

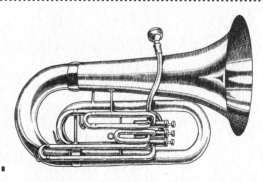

WHERE DO YOU FIND A COW WITH NO LEGS? RIGHT WHERE YOU LEFT IT.

DID YOU HEAR ABOUT THE TWO GUYS THAT STOLE A CALENDAR? THEY EACH GOT SIX MONTHS.

I'M READING A BOOK ABOUT ANTI-GRAVITY... IT'S IMPOSSIBLE TO PUT DOWN.

WHAT DO YOU CALL AN EXPLOSIVE HORSE? NEIGH-PALM.

WHY DID THE CAT RUN AWAY FROM THE TREE? BECAUSE OF ITS BARK.

WHAT HAS MORE LIVES THAN A CAT? A FROG BECAUSE IT CROAKS EVERY NIGHT.